3-15-73

CEREBRATIONS ON COMING ALIVE

CEREBRATIONS ON COMING ALIVE

**reflections in mini-forms
through behavioral theology**

WILLIAM K. McELVANEY

ABINGDON PRESS

Nashville   **New York**

Library of Congress Cataloging in Publication Data
McELVANEY, WILLIAM K. 1928-

Cerebrations on coming alive. 1. Christian life—
Methodist authors. I. Title.
BV4501.2.M233 248'.48'71 72-10669

ISBN 0-687-04826-5

Scripture quotations noted RSV are from the Revised Standard
Version of the Bible, copyrighted 1946 and 1952 by the Division
of Christian Education, National Council of Churches, and are
used by permission.

Scripture quotations noted NEB are from the New English Bible,
copyright © the Delegates of the Oxford University Press and
the Syndics of the Cambridge University Press, 1961, 1970.

Quotations of Nena O'Neill and George O'Neill are from
Open Marriage (New York: M. Evans, 1972); those of Kahlil
Gibran are reprinted from THE PROPHET, with permission of
the publisher, Alfred A. Knopf, Inc. Copyright 1923 by Kahlil
Gibran, renewal copyright 1951 by Administrators G.T.A. of
Kahlil Gibran, and by Mary G. Gibran; those of Virginia Satir
are from Conjoint Family Therapy (Palo Alto, Calif.: Science &
Behavior Books, 1967).

MANUFACTURED BY THE PARTHENON PRESS AT
NASHVILLE, TENNESSEE, UNITED STATES OF AMERICA

1755875

To the Congregation
of Northaven United Methodist Church

a community always in
process of coming alive

PREFACE AND ACKNOWLEDGMENTS

Cerebration is brain action. To cerebrate is to think. In this book I have attempted to hold forth images that will prompt you to think with greater care and insight about coming alive during the time of your life. Many of these cerebrations have first passed through my own life—and are still there—on the visceral level as well as on the cerebrational. If some of these are painful to you, I can only say, "Welcome to the struggle."

My theological roots will be obvious since I believe that God is the Life Reality calling forth human beings to be-ing and coming alive. In religious language it is God who calls the Human Being out of hiding, out of evasive rationalizations, out of patterns of escape and illusion. It is God who calls us into alive relationships and mature responsibility, with all the inevitable risks. The theme of coming alive to self, to others, to all of life, to God is central to the biblical message. The search for full and alive humanness represents, in one way or another, the universal struggle and hope of mankind.

My indebtedness to data from the behavioral sciences will also be obvious. There is too much wisdom and insight available about human beings in the behavioral fields for the church either to ignore or deny. Unfortunately, churchmen have too often made false distinctions between sacred and secular, and have been content to mumble shibboleths like "the family that prays together stays together," disregarding the actual dynamics of family interaction. In my own experience as a person and as a pastor, mature theology and sound behavioral knowledge are therapeutic companions rather than ideological competitors. The blend of the two is what I mean by behavioral theology.

In a previous writing, *The Saving Possibility* (Nashville: Abingdon, 1971), a chapter entitled "The Gospel as Life Affirmed" (subtitled "contours of celebration") made use of the impressionistic style of this present book. The enthusiastic response has encouraged me to venture forth again in a similar style. Here I have wrapped this method around four central concerns: the self, the marriage covenant, the family, and the faith community. It will be apparent that statements about these four categories are in actuality frequently more or less interchangeable. Thus, what is said about the self coming alive will frequently apply to the marriage relationship or the faith community, and vice versa, etc. Also, it will be recognized that in today's changing society, terms like "family" carry diverse connotations. The primary thrust of the vignettes on the family assumes that the term family includes both adults and children.

I acknowledge on this occasion several persons who have helped to shape my cerebrating in each of the four chapters. My self-understanding has been magnified through many relationships in the congregation of Northaven United Methodist Church, to whom this book is dedicated. Fran, Shannon, and John McElvaney constitute the marriage and immediate family community with whom I am privileged to cerebrate and celebrate daily the challenge of growth and aliveness. Our "nuclear" family has been greatly enriched and extended through a network of care, mutual concerns, and good times with the families of Gail and Jim Smith, Dotti and Tom Timmins, and with Ann and John Davis. From Bob Beavers I have learned much on the theoretical level concerning family health and pathology. My participation in the Community of Christ was strengthened years ago through the kindness and concern of Bishop Eugene Slater who at that time was pastor of the Polk Street Methodist Church in Amarillo, Texas. Though our paths haven't crossed nearly enough since seminary days, I express appreciation to Bill Steel for our friendship and for his contributions to my ministry.

A number of persons have specifically encouraged me to continue the discipline of writing. One of the persons is Bishop W. Kenneth Pope. For the typing of this "Dionysian" manuscript, thanks to Barbara Gregory for preparatory work and to Dotti Timmins for various revisions and for the final manuscript.

CONTENTS

CHAPTER 1——THE SELF COMING ALIVE ——13
CHAPTER 2——THE FEMALE-MALE
                COMMUNITY ALIVE ——49
CHAPTER 3——THE FAMILY COMMUNITY
                ALIVE ——75
CHAPTER 4——THE FAITH COMMUNITY
                ALIVE ——101

CHAPTER ONE

THE SELF
COMING
ALIVE

Coming Alive is When . . .

you LET GO

*of whatever it is in life that
you cannot let go*

*and thus receive life
back again on the new
terms of a gracious*

GIFT

Coming Alive is When . . .

you can distinguish between optimism
and hope

optimism has to do with empirical calcula-
tions, with weighing the appearance
of things, with surveying the scene

hope is a mode of perception and
discernment which goes beyond
optimism and pessimism, beyond
our capacity to make the world
come out right. hope is an expression of the fully human and thus
goes beyond humanism

we can live without
optimism
but not without hope

Coming Alive is When . . .

the greatest reward you can experience is the reward of BECOMING A HUMAN BEING . . .
>   a   growing
>   giving
>   receiving
>   caring
>   loving

>   person, becoming your deepest
>   self for others.

after all, this is what it means to glorify God. the reward of becoming a human being is THE ONLY REWARD WHICH CAN CONSISTENTLY PULL YOUR LIFE TOGETHER, THE ONLY REWARD FOR WHICH THERE IS NO SUBSTITUTE.

if this reward turns you on, excites you, challenges you, authenticates itself to you, you are alive and becoming.

if this reward is not enough, you are for the time being lost and dead to your real life.

>   what you can contribute to life may
>   seem like only a drop in the bucket
>   when seen against the total back-
>   drop of the world. but that drop in
>   the bucket is all-important and
>   ever-lastingly significant to you and
>   to the world and to God. that drop
>   in the bucket is "where it's at," the
>   difference between life and death,
>   passion and stagnation, hope and
>   despair.

Coming Alive is When . . .

we
can
find

      signs   *in the midst of suffering*
      of
      life

yet

without
lessening   *to alleviate and eliminate*
our   *suffering*
desire

To believe that there are no redemptive possibilities in suffering is to rob those who face inevitable suffering of their greatest hope and dignity.

To not strive for prevention, alleviation, and elimination of suffering is finally to be insensitive to both man and God.

Coming
Alive
is
When . . .

there
are
just
not
enough
hours
in
the
day

to see   to do

to smell

to think

to taste

to feel

to relate   to hear

to BE
to
ME

Coming Alive is When . . .

we give more than a safe, platitudinous
lip service to the cause of PEACE

<pre>
           i
           n
           f
           l
           u
           e
           n
           c   m
      r e p u t a t i o n
           i   n
           m   e
           e   y
</pre>

everyone is for peace ASLONGAS

it is an abstract ideal

*only a few are for the peace that
requires more than reciprocity,
for the peace that transcends
nationalism's pride, for the peace
that demands a universal
consciousness, for the peace that
threatens our war-based economy.*

                                        **Coming
                                         alive
                                          is
                                          when . . .**

        Conflict
              becomes

    a
        source
          of
        growth
      more
        than

                          a
          threat
            or
defeat

in conflict we have the core of our being tested.
in conflict our values are audited. in conflict we
can learn that others can disagree with us and still
respect us and even love us! in conflict we can
learn how to manage the ambivalent and the
ambiguous. in conflict we can learn our separateness and that we cannot really control others, nor
can they control us. in conflict we can discover
our own neurotic tendencies more clearly and deal
with them for what they are. in conflict we can
learn the cost and the courage of giving concre-
tion to the Gospel.

COMINGALIVEISWHEN . . .

"*worldly standards have ceased*
to count in our estimate of any man"
(II Cor. 5:16 NEB)

if you take that seriously, your
VISION will

never be the same again

Coming Alive is When . . .

penetrating and disturbing questions

are more welcome
than

seemingly
sure
and
simple
answers

Coming Alive is When . . .

I receive care from others at the time
of a death in my family

> If you'll stand up (a friend's words as
> we sat in my study), I'll put my arm
> around you

> I share your sorrow in his death even
> as I do your celebration of his life

> May you find an even greater release
> for your love through the death of
> your father

> I tried to be with you in spirit that
> day: know that you and your family
> are remembered during the coming
> weeks

> I know that no one can feel your grief
> for you, but we are deeply saddened
> with you

> . . . and I wanted you to know that I
> am caring about you right now

CARE BEGETS CARE . . . THOSE WHO ARE
CARED ABOUT ARE MORE LIKELY TO
CARE ABOUT OTHERS

```
C
O
M
I
N
G

      A
      L
      I
      V          is
      E          when . . .
```

we rejoice that God comes not *to* us, but to
be *with* us

God *to* us is the fictitious God of our
less-than-adult expectations, the God
who is expected to overcome the limits of
our existence, the God who will provide
short cuts and easy outs.

God *with* us is the One Who
Comes, the Here-and-Now Life
Possibility, the Radical Question-
er, the Liberating Word who opens
our prisons with the invitation and
demand,
"COME OUT AND LIVE."

Coming Alive is When . . .

our **primal** response to LIFE is not
            guilt
            disgust
            fear
            hostility
            revenge
            boredom
            fatigue
            deceit
            despair
            nihilism
            manipulation
            depression
            insulation
            denial
            apathy

but

YES

and this YES-to-LIFE
may mean NO-to-LIFE-
NEGATING FORCES

Coming
Alive
is
When . . .

it dawns on you that the cruciform language of Scripture (suffering servant, sacrificial love, self-denial, and all the semantics of the cross) is not an invitation to masochism or deliberate martyrdom, but an invitation to creative concern for persons

There are three choices:

1) Being like much of the world— exploit,
   dehumanize, neglect
2) Being out of the world—drop out, be uninvolved
3) Being in but not of the world— identify with the suffering that is **already** going on— risk yourself—care about others—participate in the liberating agenda—be on the case

This third choice is the intention and invitation of all cruciform language.

```
          w
          h
Coming  Alive
          s n
```

the BALLOON

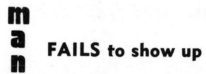 FAILS to show up

(an actual happening at 9:30 a.m.
            one Sunday morning,
but also a universal symbol)

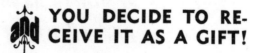 YOU DECIDE TO RE-
CEIVE IT AS A GIFT!

wewereborninthegrave
aseverychristianknows
butisalwaysforgetting
untilremindedagainand
decidedagain

*my primary drive is
not the seeking of
approval from others*

*yet I am able to
receive the approval
of others as beneficial
and enriching*

*the difference between
neurotic and healthy needs*

Coming Alive is When . . .

you are grasped by THE NEW AMBITION
which makes the human race a higher
priority than the "rat race."

*t*o the poor Jesus gave the ambition
for a new self-image and self-
determination

*t*o the affluent Jesus gave the
ambition for shared power and
reconciliation through Justice

*t*o all humanity Jesus gave

THE
NEW   AM
       BI
       TI   Ambition with
       ON   a new look!

Success
Revisited!

This is where Life
really is!

Coming Alive is When . . .

we are no longer at ease in the old dispensations, the old attitudes and habits and priorities

What happens when God happens is that the former demons no longer give what was once mistaken for life. instead we recognize them for what they are—maneuvers designed to protect us from responsible freedom.

once we've had a taste of the new wine,
the self coming alive, we can never go
back in ease, though the magnetic pull of the
old is seldom entirely absent. then we are in the
painful, celebrative discovery of the new future.

Coming
A
L
I
V
E
i s
w h
e
n . . .

faith is a lively, reckless
confidence
in the Grace of God.

~Martin Luther

31

Coming Alive is When ...

you
realize
that
the

     first
     and
     hardest
     step
     in changing

          is
          admitting
          and
          accepting

               who
               you
               are

                    R I G H T
                    N O W

(a special gift
by Nick Cole)

you say with less and less frequency, "I'll be glad when this week is over" (or when this event is past, this semester is over, or this or that has come and gone)

are you sure you're not *really* saying, "I'll be glad when LIFE is over," . . . or at least huge chunks of it that do not suit your fancy?

NEW life is NOW life. to be Christed is to live in the here and now, to become aware that life is at hand in the circumstances of the moment

The Kingdom of God
   is not
     in hand
    or
      out of hand
      but
       at hand

Christian servanthood is not equated with being servile. ❦ I find that quite a few persons try to equate these terms.

To be servile is to be cringingly submissive. ❦ Servility is a denial of God's love and of one's own worth in the light of that love. ❦ Servility is also a way in which people can manipulate and obligate others. ❦ Christian servanthood, on the other hand, is a life-style which affirms one's own significance as a person before God and mankind, and at the same time is as concerned for others as for oneself. ❦ In other words, Christian servanthood is not hung-up on obsessive pre-occupation with self, but neither does it escape the needs of the self by frenzied involvement "out there." ❦ Christian servanthood is based on a security in God through Christ, and a corresponding freedom for openness in meeting the needs of others.

1755875

we experience both the *peace*
of God and the *struggle* of
God as ours.

Peace without struggle is comfort
without challenge

Struggle without peace is challenge
without comfort

Why expect a half-loaf when God
offers a Whole Loaf?

The Gospel brings (1) torment
(2) healing (3) liberation

(1) minus (2) and (3) = graceless Judgment,
a "gospel" of guilt

(2) minus (1) and (3) = change without cost
ecstasy without agony
or faith without works

(3) minus (1) and (2) = works without faith,
feverish involvement
without abiding roots
in God's grace

For further information, see Mark 5:1-20

COMING ALIVE IS WHEN . . .

you can nod knowingly, smilingly, and joyfully to this saying from Jewish tradition: "There is no rest for the 'righteous' in this world or the next."

Coming Alive is When . . .

I can allow myself to feel my feelings, to admit to
myself when I feel depressed or anxious
or inadequate

and likewise to let out feelings of exuberance
and unmitigated joy

not everyone has this particular personal history, of course, but
if you grew up as an "underfeeler," you will know what I mean.
For others the opposite may be true. Perhaps you find growth in
developing controls over extreme highs and lows. There are manic
depressives whose feelings are like Yo-Yos, but there is also a
manic middle C with very little range either way.

Coming Alive is When . . .

care-fulness **and care-**freeness **are combined
into a unified style of life**

**be careful how you invest your life. once your
time is up, you can never get back into history
again. we become so absorbed in the** means **of
living that we lose sight of the** end **of living, thus
improving our means for unimproved ends. don't
waste your life. grow and give and live**

on the other hand

**be care-free . . . don't be so everlastingly cau-
tious and super safe. we lose our lives by trying
to guard and protect and secure them. loosen up
and live! if we secure ourselves against pain and
hurt, we also shut ourselves off from joy, from
growth, from usefulness**

Coming Alive is When . . .

you accept the fact that you're not ever going to get it all together just the way you want it. even when we're able to approximate this idyllic dream, the doubt begins to grow on us that things are so good that something is going to go wrong!

blessed are we when we can affirm life in the midst of its ambiguities and ambivalences since this is the only kind of life there is. and God's Grace offers us precisely the freedom to do so. this has to be either the best news we've ever heard or else an ultimate threat to our compulsions to be absolutely right, to be absolutely certain, and to be absolutely in control.

no wonder Jesus was crucified by some while others claimed he was the Messiah.

Coming Alive is When . . .

we
actually
realize
our
separateness
and
uniqueness,

and
also
the
capacity
for
intimate
giving
and
receiving

for
which
true
separateness
is
a
necessary
prerequisite

Coming Alive is When . . .

we
discover
it's
NOT
TOO
LATE

tolive

Coming Alive is When . . .

**the grass no longer seems
greener somewhere else**

**but in the relationships
and responsibilities which
are knocking on my
door today**

Coming Alive is When . . .

you are *freer* for selfhood, for others, for life than you used
to be

IN SPITE OF

more aches and pains
heavier lines under your eyes, greying or falling hair
more wrinkles and larger veins
and the realization that you have more past than future

you are turned on to LIFE

c
o
m
i
n
g
a
l
i
s

you get high on people

E
u
p
h
o
r
i
a

when...

Coming Alive is When . . .

I can laugh at myself

especially when someone else helps me
to do this while I'm taking myself (or my
viewpoint) with a clenched-teeth grimness

Coming Alive is When . . .

EASTER becomes the context out of which you live your life. The language of Resurrection has usually been pruned down into an unusual biological phenomenon. I believe the Resurrection—the Truth of Easter—is a much broader and more marvelous truth: namely that

> God's Grace is Irrepressible
>   and cannot be entombed or destroyed
>
> God's Grace is unfailing and undying
>
> God's Grace is alive and well

Theologians have claimed that the entire Christian faith hinges on the reality of the Resurrection. If we mean by Resurrection—and I think we should—that God's Grace is **irrepressible,** yes indeed, this is the very cornerstone of the Gospel, and Christian faith does hinge here. We are speaking now of the recurring theme of Scripture, the most basic claim of Christian faith.

> Grace is that reality which frees us from our past for a new future, which keeps presenting us with the gift of a saving possibility

> Christian satori is when some part of me is able to realize that nothing in creation can destroy or overcome God's Irrepressible Grace

Coming Alive is When . . .

you can rejoice at the accomplishments
and recognition of others

you do not have to insinuate ill of others
in order to feel good about yourself

you do not have to resort to sour grapes
in order to justify yourself

FREEATLAST

C   A
O   L
MING   IVE

 I W
 S H
    EN . . .

the foolishness of God strikes you as the ultimate
wisdom and power. All Christian symbols—from crib
to cross—possess this lowly but ultimate character,
a quality which makes you want to shout for joy and
weep at the same time.

for—

God chose what is foolish in the world to shame the
wise

God chose what is weak in the world to shame the
strong

God chose what is low and despised in the world to
overthrow the existing order

**(I Cor. 1:27-28
RSV and NEB combined)**

CHAPTER TWO

THE FEMALE-MALE

COMMUNITY

A

L

I

V

E

Coming Alive is When...

our
relationship
is
based
on

trust

respect   openness

honesty

and mutual liking

instead of

musts
oughts
shoulds
society's expectations
**our expectations based on society's expec-
tations**

50

Coming Alive is When . . .

you put the same kind of creativity and imagination
and concern

into your

M A R R I A G E
S

Y
O
U

D
O

I
N
T
O

Y
O
U
R

         J   W
P R O F E S S I O N
         B   R
                       K

you either starve your marriage
or
you feed your marriage

which do you?

Coming Alive is When . . .

WE ARE NO LONGER CULTURALLY
CONDITIONED BY AUTOMATICALLY DE-
FINING HUMAN TRAITS AS EXCLUSIVELY
MALE OR FEMALE

MEN CAN BE TENDER, GEN-
TLE, EMPATHETIC, AND NURTURING,
UNLESS BRAINWASHED BY THE STEREO-
TYPES OF SOCIETY

WOMEN CAN BE PRACTICAL,
AGGRESSIVE, EFFECTIVE, AND SELF-CON-
FIDENT, IN SPITE OF THE CULTURAL
CONSPIRACY TO THE CONTRARY

THE QUESTION BEFORE US IS NOT
WHETHER A CERTAIN TRAIT IS MASCULINE
OR FEMININE BY SOMEBODY ELSE'S AB-
SURD DEFINITION, BUT . . .

WHAT DO YOU FEEL?
WHAT CAN YOU DO?
WHY SETTLE FOR HALF YOUR
HUMANNESS AS A MALE
OR FEMALE?

WHO SAYS LITTLE BOYS MUST
NOT CRY?
WHO SAYS LITTTLE GIRLS
MUST BE WEAK AND
DEPENDENT?

Coming Alive is When . . .

    you view your marriage as a *process*
                       with
                       each
                       other

        rather than a *possession*
                       of
                       each
                       other

      rather than a *partnership*
                     with
                     rigidly
                     defined
                     roles
                     that
                     cannot
                     be
                     changed

the *process* of

    experiencing closeness without possessiveness discovering how to intertwine freedom and relatedness enabling each other toward a deeper sense of self for others utilizing conflict for growth instead of oneupsmanship

53

Coming Alive is When . . .

Intimacy
 is not a demand, but a gift to be given and received

Intimacy
 is not that which occurs only in sexual intercourse . . .
indeed intimacy can be entirely missing from physical
involvement

      Intimacy has to do with the quality
    and health of the total relationship

Intimacy involves

  awareness   openness
  care   being with
  concern   being present to

 Intimacy has to do with sharing deepest needs and hopes
. . . with meeting another center to center . . . with depth listening and depth vision . . . with the joy of touching and embracing
. . . with the capacity for a variety of mutually acceptable ways
in which two persons can choreograph their relationship

most of us are conditioned against intimacy

I expect it comes easily for only a very few, if any

we fear its claim on us, yet desire it with deep longing

Coming Alive is When ...

a marriage that has lapsed into a mere
economic and social **ARRANGEMENT**

or which is characterized by symbiotic
ATTACHMENT

becomes an **ENABLEMENT** for
personal and mutual growth

a life-giving marriage is bound
to mean that we experience many
different marriages with the same
person in order to become who we can
become. otherwise, two persons are
trapped in their past and have no
new future together.

when we got married we naively
thought the most exciting
prospect was based on who we
were at that time. thank God for
that because it brought us
together. thank God, too, that
we were wrong, because the real
excitement has come through who
we have become and are always
still becoming.

we have experienced
many marriages together. all of this
means that when we marry, we are almost
certainly marrying a person who will be
quite different in many ways than the
person we are marrying. the essential
question is whether or not these unknown
and inevitable changes-to-be become
destructive or constructive

Coming Alive is When . . .

you call into question the Masculine Mystique

the absurdly labeled "self-made man" for whom it is shameful to admit needs. for whom it is a disgrace to fail. for whom weakness is a death. the so-called rugged individual who is dependent on dependent women, whose manliness is archaic and primitive since it depends on suppression of women and the defeat of other men. the hypermanliness for whom children are women's domain.

and

you call into question the Feminine Mystique

and that means the cultural conditioning which would lead us to believe that women are innately passive (or should be!), dependent, unpredictably emotional and irrational, and desirous of securing their identity as satellites and accessories of their husbands

Today many couples are discovering a new fact about their relationship:

a *Mystique* plus a *Mystique equals* a *Mistake* in terms of human potential and healthy patterns of relationship. the combination of two mystiques is a formula for exploitation, manipulation, hostility, and the reinforcement of excessive dependency needs for both persons. Once the mystiques begin to be replaced with the new male and female humanness —and let no one underestimate the difficulty of this struggle toward a New Future—real intimacy can begin to occur.

In Jesus Christ there are neither male nor female mystiques, but male and female human beings.

56

Coming Alive is When . . .

two persons begin to realize that they married each other's neurotic defenses as well as each other's strengths (an unconscious selective vision which functions on the modus operandi, "Don't you disturb my neurosis and I won't disturb yours")

and begin to struggle out of the insecure security of our bondage toward the risk-filled possibility of change and growth

you can stay in Egypt and settle for surrender of self and freedom . . . here there is a womblike protection . . . but the view is limited

or

you can exodus into the beckoning of a new future, a new human hope . . . and then go back to Egypt where Pharaoh will take care of you

or

you can exodus into the unknown wilderness and discover a Promised Land of identity, maturity, and perpetual struggle filled with pain and joy, agony and ecstacy, dying and coming alive again, challenge and change

after all, who ever promised you a rose garden in the name of LIFE?

Coming Alive is When . . .

the death of a relationship gives birth to a new
relationship

sometimes between the same persons who are no
longer the same persons

sometimes with yourself

sometimes with life

Coming Alive is When . . .

you accept responsibility

for your own feelings and thoughts

instead of
    denying that your feelings and thoughts
        are what they are
    or blaming each other for the way you
        feel and think

Coming Alive is When . . .

it becomes clear that marriage is when

 become 1

1   in a mutual search and struggle to grow

1   in the effort to reinforce and support each other's separate identities in an intimate relationship

1   in the commitment to give and receive so as to actualize the human potential in the relationship

but **NOT** 1 in the sense of a single identity for two persons . . . <u>that</u> is the problem, not the "solution."

Coming Alive is When...

growing together

is
not
a
euphemism
for
denying
individual

feelings
growth
freedom
potential

but is an enhancement of each
other's identity and sense of self
which becomes the basis for mutu-
al enrichment and fulfillment

Coming Alive is When . . .

therelationshipitselfisthecentralfocus

insteadoffutureplansanddreams

**thenowisallyouhave.ifyousacrificeitforthefuturethe
futurewillnevercome.oritwillcomeandyouwillnot
realizeit**

**N E W   L I F E
      I S
N O W   L I F E**

Coming Alive is When...

we
know
deep
inside

that marriage is not

BE-LONGING

TO each other

but BE-COMING
WITH each other

Coming Alive is When . . .

we can accept and even rejoice in the fact that we cannot meet all of each other's needs

it's tiring and not very satisfying to be everything and everybody to another person

Coming Alive is When . . .

the growth and goals of your spouse
as a person are really important to you.

too many marriages are restrictive and possessive in
that one spouse sees the "coming alive" of the other as a
threat instead of as a gift. the adult in us will welcome
additional gifts of shared insight and experience.

the need for privacy is treated as a normal human need instead of as a rejection of togetherness

those who cannot abide solitude cannot discover beautiful togetherness

Coming Alive is When ...

Coming Alive is When . . .

re-establishing community

is more important

t
h
a
n

F
SAVI N
C   G
E

Coming Alive is When . . .

duologue

turns

into

dialogue

"In a duologue two people dutifully take turns expounding their separate lonely litanies . . . each is listening to himself rather than to the other. Susan is concerned about the cost of the braces, as well as their nuisance value, and Mark is concerned about what a merger might mean to his position in the company. Since Mark will have to pay for Bobby's braces, and since Susan will also be affected if Mark's job situation changes, they will eventually have to stop their separate soliloquies, and start all over again asking one another to repeat what has already been said. We have all been through it a thousand times."

"In open marriage if you really do not want to listen, at a given moment, it is possible for you to make that desire known to your mate, and you can expect to have your desire respected. But if your mate is going to continue to respect your desire for such moments of privacy, then you must be prepared really to listen when you indicate a willingness to do so. You must be prepared to enter into a dialogue, as opposed to a duologue. Kaplan describes the true dialogue, in which both partners listen and respond to one another, as communion rather than communication. In a true dialogue, each partner is, certainly, communicating with the other, but because he is also listening, and responding to what he hears, the final result is a form of communion."

—Nena O'Neill and George O'Neill with credits to Abraham Kaplan

Coming Alive is When . . .

anger
is
focused
on
the
issue
at
hand
instead
of
on
yesterday's
failures
or
on
some
other
question

69

Coming Alive is When . . .

the part is seen
in relation to the whole

I find this to be a very significant principle in all relationships. Do we evaluate the whole by the part or the part by the whole? When we experience disappointment or hurt, do we see everything in that context? Or do we see this in relation to the whole relationship? Only a flawless, utopian relationship could withstand the judging of the whole by the part since every part would have to be perfect.

you don't HAVE to get away from it all

*or have some super special situation in order
to enjoy each other or to break some new
ground in your relationship*

Coming Alive is When . . .

Coming Alive is When . . .

        our awareness of self and each
other gives us a knack for appropriate
TIMING

        for everything there is a
season . . .

a time to level, and a time to be
silent

a time to discuss problems and a time
to relax

a time to share bad news and a time to
wait

a time to raise questions and a time
to let it go

a time to listen and a time to speak

a time for anger and a time for
embracing

a time for humor and a time for
sobriety

TIMING is a skill which can be
developed. It can be used to
manipulate, but it can also be used
for rapport, for building up the
relationship, for a way of caring.

Coming Alive is When...

we
help each
other
to like our
bodies 🙰

to overcome
fear and loss of
confidence

to affirm the
goodness of human sexuality

to know each other

we would rather get it
out in the open
    and   face it
        deal with it
        discuss it
        cuss it

or whatever is neces-
sary to keep it from
lurking in the hidden
unexamined depths
where it festers and
pollutes

CHAPTER THREE

THE
FAMILY
COMMUNITY
ALIVE

Coming Alive is When . . .

the strongest emotional coalition

and the greatest focus of strength
within the family

is clearly in the adult marriage

where this is not true,

BEWARE OF

confused and evasive lines of communication free-floating and unrecognized neurotic needs over-investment of the mother
in the lives of the children use of the
child by the parents as a weapon against
one another

or a
triangular
power
struggle

Coming Alive is When . . .

there
is
freedom
and
openness
to
deal
with   anger and hostility

where warmth and caring predominate

a family
can develop confidence
that alienations are overcomeable
that it isn't too risky to talk about feelings
that feelings and actions are not synonymous

Coming Alive is When . . .

parents are not afraid to define clear limits when necessary

nor afraid to share the decision-making power

love sets limits, yet does so in behalf of enablement
rather than enforcement for its own sake

love sets limits, yet prefers shared power
rather than unilateral power

love uses power to grow autonomous potential
rather than paternalistic—maternalistic control

Our children don't exist to

fulfill our frustrated dreams or be our extensions
perpetuate our values, our customs, our ways
make us happy in our old age or to justify all of our "sacrifices"
substitute for other relationships we'd like to have
become scapegoats or targets for our uncomfortable feelings

"Your children are not your children.
They are the sons and daughters of Life's longing for itself.
They come through you but not from you,
And though they are with you yet they belong not to you.
You may give them your love but not your thoughts,
For they have their own thoughts.
You may house their bodies but not their souls,
For their souls dwell in the house of tomorrow, which you
cannot visit, not even in your dreams.
You may strive to be like them, but seek not to make
them like you."

—Kahlil Gibran

78

Coming Alive is When . . .

l
o
v
e

prompts

GROWTH   *rather than* *CONTROL*

AUTONOMY   *rather than* *DEPENDENCE*

ACCEPTANCE *rather than* *REJECTION*

Coming Alive is When . . .

afamilycanreachbeyonditsownneeds

and thus embrace needs of the larger human community

we cannot be satisfied
merely to gratify our
own nuclear needs

we can see ourselves
as an extended family,
extending our concerns
to all of our relatives

indeed, one of our needs I S to embrace the
struggle of the whole human family.

what are we teaching our children when . . .
they sense in us a real care for all children

decisions are made in a way that reflects our
responsibility to others

they sense that human beings of all colors and
places and backgrounds are important

the family is seen in a larger context of relationships and meanings

the family without an extended vision is
a family living in poverty . . . a poverty of life
style, of imagination, of self-image.

Coming Alive is When . . .

ADULTS CAN STEP OUT OF THEIR UL-
CERIZED, OVERPROGRAMMED, OVERCON-
TROLLED "CIVILIZATION"

INTO THAT STRANGE WORLD WHICH WE
LEFT SO LONG AGO . . . A WORLD OF WONDER
AND MAGIC, OF TREASURE AND PLEASURE,
OF PLAY AND FANTASY, OF "AHA" EXPERI-
ENCES

CHILDREN OFFER US A POINT OF CONTACT
WITH A CHUNK OF OUR SALVATION, A SALVA-
TION BASED ON RECEIVING LIFE AS A DAY-TO-
DAY GIFT

> HAVE YOU EVER NOTICED
> WHAT HAPPENS ON A CROWDED
> ELEVATOR OF GRIM, COMPULSIVE-
> LOOKING ADULTS WHEN SOMEONE
> HAS A SMALL BABY ALONG? FOR A
> BRIEF, FLEETING MOMENT, THE
> ADULTS COME OUT OF THEIR
> WORLD AND TOUCH BASE WITH
> THAT OTHER WORLD . . . THE
> WORLD THAT IS NOT ALREADY PRE-
> DICTABLE AND SEALED-IN, THE
> WORLD OF INFINITE FRESH POSSI-
> BILITIES, THE WORLD OF HUMAN
> TO HUMAN.

81

Coming Alive is When . . .

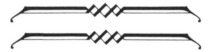

there are separate and unique selves
who can nevertheless suffer together
if one suffers and rejoice together
when one rejoices

the differentiation of selves is indispensable. yet
in the current emphasis on autonomy I wonder sometimes if we are undervaluing the significant way in
which human beings who are close can empathize
and identify with each other. autonomy should not
mean absence of care and risk and being deeply
affected by what happens to others. autonomy means
liberation for being deeply human as a unique self
in relation to other unique selves.

82

Coming Alive is When . . .

We remember how to give strokes and affirmation to one another.

Do we know how to say no to a certain form of behavior and yes to the person in spite of the behavior? Can we be honest and reveal our anger and yet say yes to the worth of the individual? Can we affirm the other's self-respect and need for good feelings about selfhood? Can we communicate "You are OK," even when you're not OK?

of course we cannot be this mature all the time, but we can strive for awareness . . . we can learn how to give strokes genuinely if we want to . . . we can grow enough to outweigh the not-OK with the OK.

where do so many people get such a low self-esteem?

why do we so often judge and try to "correct" the feelings of others instead of affirming these feelings as being real?

Coming Alive is When . . .

we recognize that GENERATION GAP which is seldom brought
to the surface

Two Worlds in Collision

World of Small Child	World of Big Adult
no concept of time	clock-oriented

Results: "Don't you realize your car pool will be here any minute, and you're not ready!"

embryonic conscience (at best)   right and wrong supposedly clearly defined

Results: "You know better than that!" or "That child doesn't ever tell the truth!"

reality limited to immediate perception   expanded view of the real

Results: "I just don't understand why he cries every time his mother gets out of sight."

does not link cause and effect   expectations based on cause and effect

Results: "That child is just stupid. She just doesn't understand anything."

feelings are natural   feelings are suspect
Results: "Just get up. You are not hurt!"

gratification of needs   right manners and being good

Results: "You are not going to leave this party until you tell Mrs. Smith what a good time you've had."

whosoever cannot learn from small child grows late early
—Contemporary Western Proverb

84

we don't expect others to read our minds

in an alive family there is a growing capacity to express needs instead of expecting others somehow just to know what our needs are

C
O
M
I
N
G

A
L
I
V
E

I
S

W   5 and 7 year old children
H   are related to
E   NOT as though they were
N . . .   babies or adults but
             as though they were
           5 and 7 year old children

Coming Alive is When...

upon occasion, at least

we receive the coming
day as a

REMARKABLE
WONDROUS
MIRACULOUS

gift

the forerunner of that time when,
for the first time, we will never be
together again under the same roof

the early harbinger of that future
moment in time when we will never
be all together again because at least
one of us will have used up his al-
lotment of time

who has gazed upon the sleeping face of his child in
the early night or morn and not been utterly aston-
ished at the miracle of life, of breath, of vital energy
which slumbers there?

Coming Alive is When . . .

our children are treated with as much respect
by parents as we would offer to other adults

and when we can forgive ourselves
for dehumanizing our children

whatever latent neurotic tendencies may be harbored in
adults will be tested by children. for though we live in
the same house, they march to a different drummer than
we do because they are children, and because they are
persons seeking their own identity. children teach us
how loving and caring we can become. and how oppres-
sive and controlling we can be. they are in-residence
educators from whom we learn about our deepest identity.

Coming Alive is When . . .

parents validate a child's need
to esteem himself in two areas:

as a masterful person

the ability to make decisions
to reason and to create
to form and maintain relationships
to time needs in relation to reality
to plan ahead
to tolerate failure and disappointment

as a sexual person

(parents mainly validate a child's
sexuality by serving as models of
a functional, gratifying male-
female relationship)

—Virginia Satir

89

Coming Alive is When . . .

the interactions within the family
tend to encourage

FEEDBACK

FEEDBACK means that

we desire to be open and clear in
communication

we acknowledge the differentiation
between any two or more persons,
that is, that no one thinks and
hears and speaks exactly like
we do

we are willing to have revealed to
us the incompleteness and fuzzi-
ness of our modes of expression

we are willing to grow in our awareness of ourselves and of our means
of communicating

both the sender and the receiver of a message
have a responsibility in the process

Coming Alive is When . . .

we
experience
as
a
family
playfulness
together

how   do   you   play   together?

```
                                            b
                                            i
                                            c
                                            y
                                            c
                                            l
                        c        e
                      g a m e s
                          m
                          p
                    k i t e s
                  p i c n i c s
                          g
```

the family that plays together . . .

is likely to discover, when the time comes,
that the children leave the nest with some
good feelings about their original family

Coming Alive is When . . .

members of a family develop ego boundaries
that are clear and well defined rather than
evasive, shifting, and prone to invade others

where this exists there is a community of separate persons
    in relationship rather than an undefined ego mass
where this exists the members do not need a stranglehold
    on one another
where this exists there can be respect for differences
    and variety
where this exists family members can relate to one another
    without being submerged in one another
where this exists there is no need to control the thoughts
    and feelings of others

if you do not experience yourself as a separate,
autonomous self, you cannot experience others as
selves

you cannot experience togetherness if there is no separateness to bring together. if there has never been
separateness, then what you have is not togetherness but
unrealized identity

the families that clutch one another for dear life
are the families with the least degree of closeness
because there is little individuality to come close

Coming Alive is When . . .

a family is Apollonian enough to grow toward intentionality,
clear expectations, consistent communication patterns, and a
rational form and order necessary for fulfillment


```
                            a      enough
           i           i   n
   and   D     n    s
           o    y
```

```
  to ex
     p
     erience a                  un
              n   emb      the predicta
              d     r                 b
                   ace                le
```

```
     the e                       the Except
         cstat                            i
           ic                             o
                                 n to the rule
```

```
  the cry
       ofthesubjective        the  immediate  need
                                 of the now
```

```
                              y
                         i   n   s   a
        the Apollonian without the  D  o       i  n
```

is grim law and order without joyful élan and freedom to
color outside the lines

the Dionysian without the Apollonian is chaotic instability,
energy without direction

Coming Alive is When . . .

**what
happens
to
one
member
of
the
family
makes
an
important
difference
to
all
of
us**

**the family is our first micro-
cosm of the universe. if it
feels   basically   supportive
and trustworthy, the whole
universe is more inviting**

Coming
   Alive
    is
     When . . .

"family" means more than biology

how about "family" as humanology?

Coming Alive is When . . .

two or more families
relate in a way that
makes possible

> *a network of care*
> *and support*
> *a multiplying of*
> *knowledge and insight*

wider experience of parenting
extended adult models for the children
a community of mutual celebration
a sharing of parental responsibilities

a human structure which enables a more di-
versified use of time and talents

Coming alive

is believed to be
what a family is
all about

it never
just happens

Coming Alive is When . . .

mistakes and errors are not treated as

FELONIES

but as a FOCUS

on a learning opportunity

we can grow Human Beings through our response
to their mistakes, or we can sentence them
to imprisonment behind the walls of self-rejection

Coming Alive is When . . .

in some sudden shaft of revelatory light

we perceive our family members not
merely as those with whom we eat and
sleep and travel and talk and laugh
and argue and agree and touch . . .

but also as totally unique persons who struggle
and search for identity, for acceptance, for their
place in the sun

in these moments we know again
the beauty and the mystery of
closeness and apartness, of
intimacy and separateness, of
youness and meness.

Coming Alive is When . . .

L
O
V
E does not require
agreement

CHAPTER 4

THE FAITH
COMMUNITY
A
L
I
V
E

the Community of Christ

is a Word-bearing change agent which exists both to bear the Word of Good News about the source, meaning, and destiny of life, and out of that Word to serve as an agent of liberating individual and social change.

the Church is more than a vision-keeper and proclaimer

the Church is more than a social action organization.

it is a community of both Word and Deed, the two being so inseparable that we might spell it out as the community of the

wordeed

Coming Alive is When . . .

Celebration is not denial of evil, death,
or suffering
not the flip side of the
manic depressive
not Easter without Good
Friday

but a profound at-one-ment with life in
its total agony and ecstasy

an affirmation that love, truth, and grace
can never be destroyed or overcome

```
        C
   G   A
   R   R
  PEACE
   J  C
  LOVE
    Y
```

GOD'S GRAFFITI — INSCRIBED ON THE
TERRAIN OF ALL LIFE

Coming Alive is When . . .

we accept our common lot with all

   the hungry
   the frustrated
   the wounded
   the isolated
   the insulted

 people of this world for the sake
of our COMMON REDEMPTION

    The liberation of another human being is my liberation too. And yours. And this liberation is both in terms of self-image and in terms of change in structures, institutions and the use of power. The Jesus Christ understanding of life enables us to welcome the gifts to history of all other human beings.

    Because in Jesus Christ we do not have to elevate ourselves by suppressing others. We are free to rejoice in the total human fulfillment. From this perspective we see other human gifts and sharing in the total societal power as contributive rather than competitive, as an enrichment of life and self rather than a diminution.

Coming Alive is When . . .

a congregation is truly supportive
in time of LOSS of

life   job

health

hopes

goals   relationship

self-respect

status

home

support has many shapes

presence

gestures

touch   words

deeds

community

Coming Alive is When...

renewal is seen not as a particular phenomenon of the church today, but as the unending task of the church in its response to the Gospel. renewal is the continuing necessity of all structures and human beings.

renewal is centered in the Word itself, but we are wising up to the fact that we also need expertise in goal-setting, frustration management, strategy-planning, and evaluation methods.

the first step out of the grave is to know when we are dead. then we can make some lifelike moves.

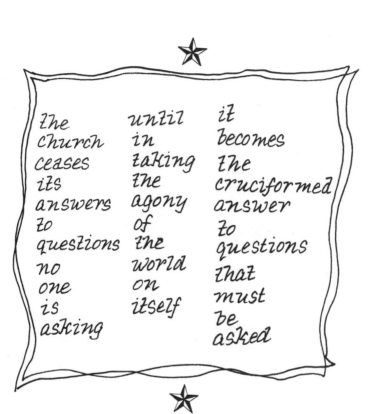

the church ceases its answers to questions no one is asking until in taking the agony of the world on itself it becomes the cruciformed answer to questions that must be asked

Coming   Alive   is   When . . .

the Christian community holds forth
the WHOLE Gospel for the WHOLE
Person by using a whole range of communication media

The <u>Body</u> of Christ

The <u>Spirit</u> of Christ

The <u>Mind</u> of Christ

the return of dance to the worship of the
church reminds us that the Gospel is em-
bodied not only in the cognitive and the
intellectual

but also in the Visible and the Visceral

the holistic is holy

Coming Alive is When . . .

a congregation refuses to use the past
as an excuse to avoid the future

an alive congregation is not content
to do things a certain way simply because
it was done that way last year. an alive
congregation is willing to pay the price of
re-doing its tradition in order

to be faithful to the Gospel

to meet the needs of the time

otherwise our buildings and budgets, our committees and coffeepots, our
administrivia and attendance forms will make us into tired midgets

**Coming
Alive
is
When . . .**

the intersection of

p
r
p a s t o r a l
p
h   occurs
e
t
i
c

in the midst of issues we need to see
people . . . all kinds of people . . . lest we
rationalize the dehumanization of those who
stand in our way in the name of "mission"

in the midst of care for individuals we
do well to remember that care cannot become a shield from a changing world but
rather an entree into it

Coming Alive is When . . .

  we are no longer satisfied with
        "business as usual"

in the midst of a world convulsing with

```
      s
   h u m i l i a t i o n
      f           p
      f           p
   d e a t h      r
      r           e
 p a i n          s
      n           s
      g           i n j u s t i c e
                  o
                  n
```

Our "usual business" I S

  the world's needs

Our "usual business" I S

  to bring good tidings to the afflicted
  to bind up the brokenhearted
  to proclaim liberty to the captives
  and the opening of the prison to
      those who are bound
  to comfort all who mourn (Isa. 61:1-2)
    The congregation which is <u>in</u> <u>trouble</u>
    is not the one where there is conflict
    and tension due to identification with
    the agony of the world. The congrega-
    tion <u>in</u> <u>trouble</u> is the one which is
    insensitive to the Gospel's command
    to love and to bring about justice.

Coming Alive is When . . .

a congregation has the courage to review
its own employment practices and its
own use of economic stewardship

do you just hire the nearest person
or do minorities have an opportunity
to apply? many churches do not
even live up to minimal federal
regulations

do you support suppliers who do not
have active programs of equal opportunity?
do you at least look for
alternatives?

is your money
where
your mouth is?

are human criteria as
important as price
quality
service?

anyone for Project Equality?

Coming Alive is When . . .

a congregation of five hundred members

has not one or two ministers

but hundreds of ministers

who celebrate the Gospel as a corporate act
who care for one another and reach out to one another
who are about their tasks from day to day

using pulpits made out of business transactions,
relationships with neighbors and families,
classroom responsibilities, and political issues

and churches made out of highways, living rooms,
downtown offices, airplanes, kitchens, golf courses,
assembly lines, doctors' offices, bedrooms, and
grocery stores

priesthood
r
o
pastorhood
h
e
t   of all believers
h
o
o
d

pillars give way to people

recently I heard of a large congregation "pulpit committee" which had eight men on it. period. no women. no youth

in God's name, what kind of church is that?

it's sad enough that most congregations are monochromatic. we could at least utilize the diversity we do have within the diversity we don't have.

Coming Alive is When . . .

our commissions and councils are real face-to-face encounters on significant issues between persons who let it hang out and who will be open to others

the most exciting and rewarding and worthwhile board meeting I ever attended was an all-out, no-holds-barred dialogue-debate-argument-confrontation concerning the congregation's involvement in the Poor People's Campaign. Here's what the meeting meant:

1. A demonstration that we could grow through conflict, that we could agree to disagree.
2. An example of strong feelings being expressed and dealt with constructively.
3. A reminder that we win on some issues, lose on others (my point of view was an unsilent minority).

there is no question about the value of the Christian community if through it persons can increase their communication skills and awareness, and if persons can express real feelings without being ridiculed or put down. Some adults have had almost no help and practice in this kind of growth.

115

Coming Alive is When . . .

      all of our celebrative sounds and stir-
rings are offered against the backdrop of
what is going on in the world

                  as it really is . . .

"In a culture that glorifies success and happiness
and is blind to the suffering of others, remember-
ing that at the center of the Christian faith there
stands an unsuccessful, suffering, and shamefully
dying Christ can open man's eyes to the truth,
shatter the tyranny of pride and awaken solidarity
with those who are hurt and humiliated by our
culture."

                      —Jurgen Moltmann

Coming Alive is When . . .

        our language of love
            is accompanied by
            the deed of
            empowerment

        God's Grace is the reality
    of loving empowerment,
    and thus the one true church
    is whenever loving empowerment
    for human beings happens

    love minus empowerment can be
        games churchmen play

        power without love
    can be the end of the world

Coming Alive is When . . .

we intentionally alter our priorities
so that more energy, time, and resources
are directed toward the enablement of
the oppressed, the outcast, the powerless.
this will never happen accidentally but
by deliberately setting the agenda in
this direction

since most congregations already have
fixed obligations financially, such as
building payments, salaries, and utilities,
we will need to consider 2nd and 3rd
mile efforts

to whom much is given
much is required
much is possible

persons are taken as seriously

after membership

as before membership

Coming Alive is When . . .

Coming Alive is When . . .

the church lets the world in

stained glass windows are not supposed to screen out the pollution of the world nor hold in the piety of the saints. stained glass windows should remind us that the church belongs in the world, especially if they portray figures like Moses, Isaiah, Amos, Jesus, Paul, Peter, Luther, Calvin, and Wesley.

windows should also remind us of the beauty of God's world and that we cannot participate in this beauty apart from the suffering, the hostility, the alienation, the desperation.

if we shut the world out, how will God-in-Christ-in-World be present in our congregational life?

Coming Alive is When . . .

worship

suburban style

erupts out of its usual channels,
utilizing a kaleidoscope of
sounds, movements, colors,
and surprises.

we need to dance, to applaud
when we feel like it, to
loosen up and let go

of course no worship style truly comes alive if it is essentially
Gospel-less.

Coming Alive is When . . .

the CENTER of the congregation is

NOT

  absence of conflict
  pleasing personalities
  morally righteous people
  impressive facilities
  a likable and talented pastor
  a certain small group of power wielders
  an avant-garde reputation
  a secure and safe haven from change
  good attendance records
  a large staff
  a one-man show
  100 years of uninterrupted service
        to the community
  the eleven o'clock worship hour
  a strong program for children
  a rapidly growing membership

but the

G
WORD
S
P
E
L

Coming Alive is When . . .

our involvement in the Body of Christ is
undergirded in a global vision of the
church universal

this global vision senses
that many colleagues of the
spirit are about their tasks,
thus forming an international
network of the humanizing process.

the global vision reminds us of
the ancient heritage of the
community and of our representational
responsibility before mankind

the global image
reinforces the
intentionality
of our common
efforts, as well
as a sense that
we are sustained
through one another
by God's Grace

without the universal consciousness, we are more
prone to see the church as merely one suburban
agency among others . . . more likely to feel isolated
and impotent . . . less likely to be aware of the
human drama unfolding in our time and our part
in the drama

Coming Alive is When . . .

we cease to daydream about
what the church used to be
or pipedream about what we
wish we were

and begin to take a
look at what we can
do now with what God
is giving us today

is there any other place to begin?

Coming Alive is When . . .

        task groups set up their own agenda, pursue
goals, evaluate their efforts, and assume responsibility
for an area of competence

in many task groups we see the utilization
of the same kind of lay ingenuity
and imagination as one would see in
professional vocations

this is the CHURCH at work

Coming Alive is When . . .

in the midst of the GAPS

East - West

under 30 - over 30

counter culture - counter counter culture

male - female

majority - minority

w
h
i
t
e

red
black
brown
yellow

conservative - liberal

we can experience the mystery
and joy of barrier-breaking
instead of barrier-making

from <u>GAP</u> to A-<u>GAP</u>-E